25 FUN & SAFE SCIENCE EXPERIMENTS FOR KIDS

PERFECT FOR KIDS TO DO AT HOME! AGES 5-13.

DR. ESTHER ANDERSON

INTRODUCTION

Tips for doing these experiments

Read the instructions right through first
Collect everything you need before you start
Note that some experiments involve hot water or cutting things. Ask an adult to help with these
Watch carefully, maybe take photos.
Be patient! Some of the experiments take time
And (your parents will love this) clear up when you're finished.

And a word about science

Scientists are like detective. They notice things and ask questions and wonder about the world around them. And sometimes the things they notice are the start of great discoveries. Here's some examples: A famous scientist called Archimedes once noticed that when he got into the bath the water level rose and splashed over the top. It suddenly dawned on him that his body displaced a weight of water equal to the weight of his body. He leaped out of the bath and ran down the street to the King's palace, because this observation helped him solve a problem he'd been given – was the King's crown pure gold, or had a lighter metal been substituted?

Another scientist, Isaac Newton, is famous for working out the universal law of gravitation. The story is that he was sitting under an apple tree and noticed an apple fall. He didn't just think: 'So what?' He started to wonder why things always fell down towards the earth. And he realised that this was a result of a force exerted by the earth, and all other objects, and after a lot more thinking and calculating he came up with his famous theory.

Isaac Newton made many discoveries in science and maths. Not only by observing and thinking, but also by studying the ideas of great scientists of the past. He commented to a friend about his famous discoveries: 'If I have seen further than others, it is by standing upon the shoulders of giants'.

Have fun –and keep watching and thinking!

ACKNOWLEDGMENTS

Some of these experiments have been around for such a long time, it's not possible to find out who first thought of them. But many thanks to all those inventive people. Thanks to the CSIRO and many other organisations whose suggestions for science experiments have found their way online.

And a note about spelling. We'll use the US spelling, not the UK spelling, so you'll see color, not color, mold not mould etc.

LIKE FIREWORKS UNDER WATER

What you need

- A tall glass or glass jar
- Tap water
- Vegetable oil (any kind of cooking oil will do e.g. sunflower oil, safflower oil)
- Food coloring – red, yellow, green and blue (if the food coloring isn't in squeeze bottles you'll need an eye dropper or a teaspoon to add drops of food coloring)

What you do

- Fill the glass ¾ full of water
- Pour oil slowly onto the water till there's about 3 cm depth of oil floating above the water (about the length of your little fingernail
- Drop several drops of each color onto the oil
- Watch what happens
- Keep adding drops of food coloring and watch how the colors spread, until all the water is colored

What did you see?

Usually when people do this experiment they see that the drops of food coloring first form colored round beads (spheres) where the oil and water layers meet, then the colors swirl downwards in the water, mixing together in colorful patterns like fireworks in the sky. Is this what you saw?

Why does this happen? - the science behind what you saw

Oil floats on water because it is less dense (heavier) than water. The food coloring is denser than oil, so it sinks down into the water. When it is in the water it mixes with the water, and continues to spread out into the water, moving from where it is highly concentrated to where there is less coloring (low concentration). As you keep adding drops of food coloring, the colored spheres will keep dropping out of the oil, giving the water a 'fireworks' look.

A CANDLE THAT SUCKS UP WATER

What you need

- A glass
- A saucer
- Tap water
- A candle that will fit inside the glass (a tea light candle will do)
- Matches or a lighter

What you do

- Place the candle in the middle of the saucer. Fill the saucer with water.
- Light the candle (or ask an adult to light it).
- Place a glass over the candle.
- Watch carefully
- When the flame goes out, the water in the saucer will get sucked into the glass.

Why does this happen? - The science behind what you saw

When the candle is burning, the heat makes the air in the glass expand, so some of the air moves out of the glass. The candle will go out after it uses up all the oxygen in the glass, then the air inside the glass cools and the air pressure inside the glass drops. Because the air pressure outside the glass is then higher than inside the glass, the water on the saucer is forced into the glass by the higher air pressure outside.

3

STOPPING WATER FROM MIXING

You know that if you pour water from a glass into a glass that already has water in it the water will mix together. But try this experiment and watch what happens (Best do it on the kitchen bench or somewhere it doesn't matter if some water gets spilled.)

What you need

- Two identical glasses
- Tap water
- Salt
- A tablespoon
- Food coloring
- Sheet of paper

What you do

- Fill the two identical glasses with water.
- Add two tablespoons of salt to the water in one glass and stir till the salt has dissolved (so you can't see the salt any more)

- Add a few drops of food coloring to the water in the other glass.
- Put a sheet of paper on top of the glass of colored water, keep holding the paper over the glass and turn the glass upside down and place it on top of the glass of salt water.
- Very gently pull the paper out from between the glasses.
- You'll probably find that the colored water and the salt water remain separate and don't mix.

Why does this happen? - The science behind what you saw

Salt water is heavier than colored water without salt, so they stay separate as long as the boundary between them isn't disturbed.

However, if you turn the two glasses over, the salt water will be on top, and because it is heavier it will flow down and mix with the colored water.

MAKING A CRYSTAL SNOWFLAKE

What you need

- Salt
- Water
- Large glass jar
- 3 pipe cleaners (also called chenille stems)
- String
- Pencil
- Blue food coloring (optional)
- Magnifying glass (optional)

This experiment can be done using borax instead of salt, which will give you larger crystals, but WARNING! borax can be irritating to the skin, and is unhealthy if you breathe it in. Borax is sold as a cleaner in some supermarkets.

What you do

- Make a 6 pointed star shape out of the pipe cleaners by twisting them over each other so the ends stick out like the points of a star.

- Tie a piece of string round the middle of your star
- Test to see if the star will fit easily into your jar, by lowering the star into the jar. If it's too big, then trim the ends of your star so you can lower the star into the jar without squashing it. Take the star out, and tie the free end of the string to a pencil (the string should be long enough so that when the pencil is placed across the top of the jar, the star dangles freely in the jar)
- Ask an adult to make salt water by heating enough water to fill the jar and when the water starts to boil, add salt till crystals start to form in the water (this will take lots of salt).
- Let the salt water cool for a minute
- To prevent the jar cracking when hot water is added, warm the jar by filling it with warm tap water, and emptying it out. Then put a metal spoon in the glass jar and ask an adult to slowly pour the hot salt water into the jar. Take the metal spoon out (The metal spoon is there to conduct some of the heat from the water away, to prevent the glass jar from cracking, as glass can sometimes crack if hot water is added). Drop your star into the salt water, and rest the pencil on the top of the jar. Add some blue food coloring if you want a blue star.
- Leave the jar on a sunny windowsill for 3 days, then take your snowflake out and let it dry. If you have a magnifying glass, look at the crystals.
- You can then hang it up as a decoration

Why do crystals form? - The science behind what you saw

Very hot water can hold much more dissolved salt than cold water. Hot water molecules are moving very fast and are spread out which makes space available for more borax to dissolve into it. As the mixture cools, the water molecules slow down and move closer together. That means there's less room for the dissolved salt and it begins to fall out of the water.

The salt keeps settling out of the cooling suspension due to gravity, and it bonds with other salt on the pipe cleaner snowflake and begins to form crystals, as the salt molecules come together in repeated patterns. The salt keeps on falling and crystalizing on top of the snowflake until you pull it out of the jar.

CABBAGE CHEMISTRY

What you need

- Leaves from a fresh **red** cabbage cut into strips (ask an adult to do this).
- Plastic bottle with lid (e.g. clean plastic 2 litre milk container)
- Water from the hot tap
- 6 glasses
- 6 spoons
- Test solutions
- vinegar
- lemon juice
- tap water
- soapy water
- water with dishwashing liquid added
- water with washing powder or laundry liquid added

If you can't get a red cabbage, use red grape juice instead, but if you use grape juice, use cold water not hot water.

What to do

- Place the cabbage leaves in the plastic bottle, half fill the bottle with hot water (ask an adult to do this) and screw the lid on tightly.
- Shake the bottle until the water turns a purple color. This may take a few minutes. Leave it to cool.
- Place a small amount of the test solution in separate glasses (vinegar in the first glass, lemon juice in the 2nd glass, tap water in the 3rd glass, soapy water in the 4th glass, water with dishwashing liquid in the 5th glass and water with washing powder or laundry liquid in the 6th glass.
- Now half fill each cup with the red cabbage water (or diluted grape juice) and stir using a different clean spoon for each cup.
- What has happened to the color in each cup?

Why does this happen? - The science behind what you saw

Solutions can be classed as acidic, basic or neutral. Vinegar and lemon juice are acidic (vinegar is also called acetic acid, and lemon juice contains citric acid), tap water is usually neutral, and things we use for cleaning (soap, laundry powder) are usually basic. Basic substances are also called alkaline.

If you used cabbage leaves, and the color is cherry red the solution is strongly acidic, if it is pinkish-red it's acidic, if it's purple red it's slightly acidic, if it's purple it's neutral, if it's blue it's slightly basic, if it's green it's basic and if it's yellow it's strongly basic.

We say whether things are acidic, basic or neutral by using a scale called the pH scale. The pH scale ranges from 0 to 14, with 0 being a very strong acid, 7 being neutral and 13 – 14 being a very strong base.

Pure water has a pH of seven, but tap water varies from place to place, and some places have mildly alkaline tap water.

A substance that changes color when acids or bases are added is called an indicator. Red cabbage and grape juice contain chemicals that act as acid-base indicators.

6

SODA FOUNTAIN

What you need

- A 2 L bottle of a fizzy drink (soda) like lemonade or mineral water. Diet soft drink is fine. Don't use orange soft drink or Solo.
- Sugar (about half a cup or more)
- A jug or a funnel (to pour the sugar into the bottle)

Do this experiment outside

- Open the bottle of soft drink and place the bottle on the ground so it will not tip over.
- Pour the sugar quickly into the bottle and watch what happens

Why does this happen? - The science behind what you saw

The bubbles that you see in soft drink are carbon dioxide gas. While the bottle is closed, the gas can't expand to form bubbles.

When you open the bottle the gas can escape, and adding sugar provides lots of surface area for the gas bubbles to form around, so bubbles and soft drink cascade over the top of the bottle like a fountain.

Adding sand will have the same effect as adding sugar. The places where the bubbles start to form are called centres of nucleation, and the more of these there are, the more bubbles will form.

DISAPPEARING SHELL AND BOUNCY EGG

What you need

- hard-boiled egg, with shell on
- glass wide enough to hold the egg
- vinegar

What you do

- Put the egg into the vinegar. What happens?
- Leave the egg in the vinegar for at least a day. What do you see?
- Take the egg out of the vinegar and rinse it with water. Rub the shell, and the shell will rub off.
- Squeeze the egg gently and let go. Poke it gently with your finger. If should feel bouncy, like rubber.

What's happening

Vinegar is an acid (called acetic acid) and it 'eats away' the eggshell (which is made of calcium carbonate), leaving the inner membrane of the eggshell. The calcium carbonate makes the shell hard, so when it is gone the egg feels rubbery.

The bubbles you see when the egg is placed in vinegar are carbon dioxide gas. Carbon dioxide is produced by a chemical reaction between calcium carbonate (the egg shell) and acetic acid (the vinegar).

The chemical reaction keeps on going until all of the calcium carbonate in the eggshell is used up. This takes about a day.

Some rocks are made of calcium carbonate. Geologists can tell if a rock is calcium carbonate by dropping a small piece of it in acid and seeing if it produces carbon dioxide bubbles. This is called the 'acid test'.

KITCHEN VOLCANO

What you need

- A small watermelon (or pumpkin or apple)
- Vinegar
- Bicarbonate of soda (baking soda, sodium bicarbonate)
- Knife to cut a small hole in the watermelon
- Spoon or melon baller to scoop out the watermelon flesh
- Plate to put the watermelon flesh on
- Large tray to rest the empty watermelon on

This activity is best done outside or on a kitchen bench (it can be messy)

A pumpkin or apple or lemon can be used if you haven't got a watermelon. If you use a lemon, you can use lemon juice instead of vinegar

What you do

- Cut a small hole in the top of the watermelon and scoop out the insides, and put these on a plate to be eaten later.

- Pour a packet of baking soda into the hole (less if it's a very small watermelon)
- Pour vinegar into the hole and stand back and watch the eruption!
- Keep adding vinegar and baking soda to your watermelon-cano
- Adjust the amounts of vinegar and baking soda to make sure the fizzy 'lava' gushes out the top.
- You can make it frothier by adding dishwashing liquid (dish soap) and color the 'lava' red with food coloring.

Why does this happen? - The science behind what you saw

When the baking soda and the vinegar are combined a chemical reaction occurs that produces carbon dioxide gas. This is what causes your watermelon volcano to fizz.

9

THE MYSTERY OF MOLD (MOULD IN UK SPELLING)

What you need

- Five oranges
- Five saucers
- A clear plastic bag
- Whole cloves (you can buy these in the spice section of a supermarket or grocery store

What you do

- Put an orange on a saucer and leave it on a windowsill
- Put some water in a saucer, add an orange and leave on a windowsill
- Put an orange in a plastic bag, put it on a saucer and leave it on a windowsill
- Stick cloves into an orange until it is completely covered, put it on a saucer and leave it on a windowsill
- Put an orange on a saucer in the fridge
- Check each orange every day, and note when you first see mold (green or blue patches) on any of the oranges, or any other change.

- Can this experiment help you work out the best way to keep oranges from becoming moldy?

The science behind what you saw

Molds are fungi that are often found growing on food. You can tell if food is going moldy because you'll see coloured patches appear on the surface, and the food often becomes more squashy and mushy, and sometimes fluid leaks out from it . The green/blue colour of mold on oranges is caused by spores of the fungi. Spores are small and light and are carried by air currents. If they land on suitable food they'll grow into a new fungus, and cause that food to become moldy too. Some molds produce toxins that can make you sick so it's best not to eat moldy food. Molds growing in soft fruits like oranges can grow deep into the fruit, so the whole fruit shouldn't be eaten. In hard foods like carrots, if just a small patch of mold is seen, the mold may not have grown deep into the carrot and it may be safe to cut the mold patch away and eat the rest of the carrot.

So much food is wasted because it has gone moldy that scientists have spent lots of time trying to work out the best way to stop this happening.

What did you find from your experiment with oranges? What do you think is the best way from stopping an orange going moldy? Can you think of other things you could try to stop mold growing on food?

10
———

RACE TO THE TOP

If you live in a place with cold winters, wait till spring to do this experiment

What you need

- 5 apple pips (seeds)
- 5 orange or lemon or mandarin pips (seeds)
- 5 pumpkin seeds or sunflower seeds or watermelon seeds
- A tomato (the seeds are inside)
- A strawberry (the seeds are the little specks on the outside of the strawberry)
- A packet of lettuce, broccoli, cabbage or cauliflower seeds
- 6 flower pots (or plastic containers e.g. yoghurt or butter or margarine containers – ask an adult to make holes in the bottom so they are like flower pots)
- 6 plates
- Garden soil or potting mix
- Labels to stick in each pot – you can make your own by cutting a piece of white plastic from a margarine container and writing on it with permanent marker.
- Clear plastic container with lid

- Paper towel

What you do

Fill each pot with soil or potting mix, poke 5 holes in the soil with your finger or a stick, about the depth of a fingernail, and add a seed to each hole, and cover with soil (so all the apple seeds are in one pot, orange seeds in another etc.)

Put each pot on a plate, and water gently. A watering can or spray bottle is best. Stop when you see water coming out the bottom of the pot.

Leave them in a place where they'll get sunlight when they start to grow.

Cover the bottom of your plastic container with paper towel. Add water till the all the paper towel is damp. Sprinkle seeds from your seed packet onto the paper towel, put the lid on and leave in a dark place e.g. in a cupboard.

Water the plants in pots every day, and check if the seedlings have started to come up through the soil

Check the seeds in the plastic container every day to see if roots have started to form. When his happens, put the container in a place where it will get light during the day but not direct sunlight. Keep checking every day till you see leaves growing. Then you can plant the seedlings in soil in a pot, or in a garden

Which seeds were the first to grow leaves?

Which seedlings grew fastest/tallest

Why do seeds start to grow?

Seeds need water, oxygen and a suitable temperature to start growing. When a seed starts growing we say it has germinated. Different seeds germinate at different times. Things that can stop seeds germinating are: not enough water, too high or too low a temperature, too much water (that stops oxygen getting to the seed, or causes the seed to rot), being eaten by insects or other organisms in the soil.

11

MAKE YOUR OWN BATH BOMBS

What you need

- 10 tablespoons of bicarbonate of soda (sodium bicarbonate or baking soda)
- 3 tablespoons of citric acid (available from supermarkets)
- food coloring
- dried flower petals (e.g. rose petals) – optional
- sweet almond oil
- scented oil (e.g. rose oil or lavender oil)
- 2 large mixing bowls
- 1 large muffin tray or fairy cake tray
- 1 small glass jar
- rubber gloves
- spoon

What you do

- Rub the sides and bases of the muffin tray with a small amount of almond oil, (so the bath bombs won't stick to the tray
- Place the citric acid and bicarbonate of soda into a large

bowl. Mix the ingredients together well, to form the base mixture

- Scoop out about half a cup of this mixture and put it in into another bowl, and add the flower petals.
- Add 6 drops of scented oil, 5 teaspoons of sweet almond oil and about 10 drops of food coloring to the small glass jar, then mix together with a spoon
- Slowly pour the oil mixture into the half cup of mixture. Put on rubber gloves and mix it together with your hands. Keep mixing till it stays together in your hands.
- Spoon the mixture into the muffin tray and press it down firmly.
- Repeat with the rest of the mixture, using different scented oil or food coloring to make more bath bombs.
- Leave the bombs in the tray to set for a few days.
- Turn the tray upside down over a plate to remove the bombs from the moulds.
- When you next have a bath, drop one of your bath bombs in. What happens?

Why did this happen? – The science behind what you saw.

When the bath bomb dissolves in water, there is a chemical reaction between the sodium bicarbonate and citric acid that produces a chemical called sodium citrate, and also produces a gas, carbon dioxide, that causes the fizzing,

The almond oil is released from the bath bomb into the water and forms a thin layer on your skin. You should be able to smell the rose oil or lavender oil too.

12

GET DNA FROM STRAWBERRIES

DNA stands for Deoxyribonucleic Acid. It is found the cells of every living thing. DNA tells animals, plants bacteria and fungi how to grow (like an instruction manual) and is the reason why e.g. strawberries look like strawberries , and elephants look like elephants.

DNA is organized into sections called genes and is coiled around proteins to form chromosomes. You may know that genes are inherited from your parents, and are the reason why you may have, for example hair like your dad, eyes like your mum, a nose like your Grandfather or a smile like your Grandmother.

There are many reasons why scientists study DNA. DNA can be used for example, to help diagnosis hereditary diseases, to develop new medicines or vaccines or modify crop plants to resist insects. DNA can also help identify criminals.

What you need

- 3 ripe strawberries
- Measuring cup
- One third of a cup of rubbing alcohol or methylated spirits (methylated spirits can be used to clean paint brushes, so it is available from hardware stores and paint

shops. Rubbing alcohol is mainly either isopropyl alcohol or ethanol and may be available from pharmacists.)

- Teaspoon
- Tablespoon
- Half a teaspoon of salt (use non-iodized salt)
- 1 tablespoon of dishwashing liquid (dish soap, for hand-washing dishes, detergent) or shampoo
- One third cup of tap water
- Glass or small bowl to mix the extraction liquid in
- Cheesecloth, muslin, gauze or a coffee filter
- Funnel, or if you don't have a funnel, a rubber band to hold the coffee filter or gauze in place.
- Tall drinking glass
- Resealable plastic bag
- Small glass jar (such as a spice or baby food jar) or small clear plastic cup
- Clean wooden stick e.g. bamboo skewer, popsicle (icypole) stick or clean sate stick. (If you use a baby food or short spice jar, you could substitute a toothpick for the skewer.)
- Ice in a bucket (or the use of a freezer)

What you do

1. Cool the alcohol by putting it in the freezer in a plastic container (it won't freeze solid, it will just get cold), or in a plastic container in a bucket of ice

2: Mix the DNA extraction liquid (soapy, salty water)

- Put 1 tablespoon of dish detergent (washing up liquid, dish soap) in a small bowl or glass
- Slowly mix in half a teaspoon of salt.
- Add 1/3 cup of water and mix.

3: Get the DNA

- Take the green tops (sepals) off 3 strawberries (one if it's a very big strawberry) and put it into your plastic bag, push most of the air out of the bag by running your hands up the sides, and close the bag.

- Mash up the strawberry, by squishing the plastic bag in your hands until there are no big chunks of strawberry.
- Add 2 tablespoons of the DNA extraction liquid that you prepared.
- Push out the extra air, then close the bag, and continue squishing the plastic bag to mix the strawberry and extraction liquid for one minute.

4: Separate the fluids from the solids

- Line the funnel with the coffee filter (or cheesecloth or muslin or gauze) and place it over a clean glass. If you don't have a funnel, you can just hold the filter or gauze over the glass with a rubber band
- Pour the mix of strawberry and extraction liquid into the funnel and let it filter until the fluid has stopped dripping into the glass. Remove the funnel.

5: Extract the DNA

- Tip the glass slightly and gently pour down the side of the glass an approximately equal amount of cold alcohol as there is strawberry liquid. Do not mix or stir, so the alcohol sits in a layer above the strawberry liquid
- Watch for the appearance of a white substance (DNA) above the strawberry liquid layer.
- Tilt the cup and pick up the DNA using a clean wooden stick. The DNA should look like gooey, cloudy white or clear stringy stuff ,and should wrap around the stick, if you twist the stick.

How did it work?

When you added the salt and detergent mixture to the mashed strawberries, the detergent helped lyse (pop open) the strawberry cells, releasing the DNA into solution, and the salt helped remove the proteins bound to the DNA, and helped the DNA strands clump together, so they were easier to see. Ripe strawberries also have enzymes called pectinases and cellulose that help break down cell walls.

DNA is not soluble in alcohol so after you added the cold rubbing alcohol to the filtered strawberry liquid, the clumps of DNA should have precipitated out of solution and become visible. A single strand of DNA is too tiny to see without a microscope, but because lots of DNA strands clumped together it was possible to see it. Strawberries are good to use for this experiment because they have 8 copies of each chromosome in their cells, and chromosomes are made of DNA (and protein).

13

SLIME

What you need

- Cornflour
- Food coloring
- Small bowl
- Spoon
- Water

What to do

1. Pour some cornflour into a bowl.
2. Stir in small amounts of water until the cornflour becomes a very thick paste.
3. Stir about five drops of food coloring into the mixture to color it.
4. Stir your slime REALLY slowly. This should be easy.
5. Stir your slime REALLY fast. This should be almost impossible.
6. Now punch your slime REALLY hard and fast. It should feel like you're punching a solid.

The slime will keep in a fridge for several days. You'll probably need to stir it before you use it again, as the cornflour may settle.

The science behind this kind of slime

Anything that flows is called a fluid. Fluids like water which flow easily are said to have low viscosity, whereas fluids that do not flow so easily are said to have a high viscosity (like honey), or said to be very viscous (not vicious).

Cornflour slime isn't like most fluids. When pressure is applied to slime, like when you stir it very fast, its viscosity increases and the cornflour slime becomes thicker.

Cornflour slime loses its flow and behaves like a solid if it is punched. Cornflour slime is an example of a shear-thickening fluid.

There are also shear-thinning fluids that do the opposite- they get runnier when you apply pressure, e.g. toothpaste is runny when you squeeze it out of the tube, but becomes more solid on the toothbrush

14

MAKE MORE SLIMY SLIME – AND LEARN
ABOUT RUNNY NOSES

This recipe will make slime that is very like mucus or snot from your nose when you have a cold

What you need

- 1 tablespoon of unflavoured gelatine powder (from a supermarket)
- ½ cup golden syrup
- 1 tablespoon of salt
- Hot water
- Food coloring
- 2 bowls

What you do

- Place the gelatine and salt in the bowl.
- Add ½ cup of syrup.
- Add ½ cup of hot water. Add food coloring if you want it to look like green or yellow colored snot.
- Mix every thing together and put in a fridge to cool for 30 minutes.

- Run a fork through the mixture to see how runny it is. It will get thicker and thicker as it cools, if it is too thick, you can add more water. Pour it out of the bowl into the second bowl and watch how it pours. Does it look slimy? Does it look like mucus (snot) from your nose when you have a cold?

The science behind what you saw

The mixture you made looks and behaves very like mucus from your nose . Mucus is made of water, mucins (large proteins), and salts, epithelial (surface) cells, dead leukocytes (white blood cells). The mucus-like slime that you made contains water, salt and protein (gelatine is animal protein), almost like real mucus.

The gelatine dissolves in hot water making a thick solution, but won't dissolve) in cold water. When cooled, the gelatin swells to make jelly-like slime.

What does mucus do?

Mucus in your nose traps dust etc. in the air that you breath in, and are expelled from your nose when you blow your nose.

The inside of your nose is lined with membrane that produce mucus. Mucus is also produced in your sinuses, lungs, stomach and intestines.

When you get a cold, which is a viral infection in your upper respiratory tract, your body produces much more mucus than normal to carry away waste material. When you have a respiratory infection, your mucus can change color to yellow or green because of dead white blood cells and other waste carried out of your nose in the mucus.

15

MILK PUDDLE SCIENCE

What you need

- Milk
- A shallow bowl
- Food coloring (3 different colors)
- Dishwashing liquid/detergent (dish soap)
- A toothpick or cotton bud (Q-tip)

What you do

- Pour some milk into a bowl.
- Wait a few minutes then add a few drops of food coloring. What do you see?
- Add a little dish soap/detergent to a toothpick or a Q-tip, then touch the food coloring drops in the milk. What happens?

The science behind what you saw

After you added the drops of food coloring to the milk, the droplets probably stayed as little drops in the milk. But when you added the detergent, the colors will swirl around over the surface of the milk. This is because the detergent causes a chemical reaction that breaks the surface tension, allowing the colors to move.

BALLOONS AND ELECTRICITY

What you need

- 2 balloons
- Ribbon or string
- Tap water
- Piece of tissue paper (used for gift wrapping) or a few tiny scraps of writing paper
- Empty aluminum can, placed on its side

What you do

- Blow up the balloons and tie the ends with ribbon or string
- Dangle one balloon over the 2nd balloon, then over the paper, then over the empty can. Does anything happen?
- Rub both balloons against your hair till your hair starts to lift up and stick to the balloon
- Dangle one balloon over the 2nd balloon, then over the paper, then over the empty can. Does anything happen?
- Rub a balloon against your hair again till your hair starts to lift up

- Hold the balloon close to a stream of running water from the cold tap. The stream of water should bend towards the balloon.
- Rub the balloons against a woolen item e.g. a woolen sock, jumper or scarf, and .

The science behind what you saw

Rubbing the balloon onto your hair or against wool causes the balloon to become negatively charged, because the rubbing adds electrons to the ballon. When charged, the 2 balloons will move away from each other because they both have the same charge and like charges repel. Opposite charges attract. Paper, hair, aluminum can and water are positively charged so they will be attracted to the negatively charged charged balloons and move towards them.

17

LAVA LAMP IN A GLASS

What you need

- Alka Seltzer tablet (or bicarbonate of soda and citric acid)
- Vegetable oil
- Water
- Food coloring
- Tall glass or jar

What you do

1. Fill the glass with 2 inches (5cm) depth of water.
2. Add food coloring (your favourite color).
3. Add oil to almost fill the glass, but stop at about 1 inch (2.5 cm) from the top
4. Drop an antacid tablet (e.g. Alka-Seltzer tablet) into the mixture and watch

(Alka Seltzer tablets contain aspirin (a pain killer), sodium bicarbonate and citric acid. When the tablets are placed in water, sodium bicarbonate and citric acid combine to form sodium citrate, carbon dioxide, and water. The carbon dioxide bubbles move slowly through the oil, giving a larva lamp appearance

FROZEN 1

What you need

- Water in a plastic bottle chilled in the freezer till it's almost frozen
- Ice cubes
- Ceramic bowl

What you do

- ¾ fill a plastic bottle with water, put the lid on tightly and put it on its side in the freezer for about two hours (till it's almost frozen). Take it out and shake the bottle gently, if you see crystals form it's ready to use.
- Place a ceramic bowl upside down on a flat surface (e.g. next to kitchen sink, because water may spill)
- Place an ice cube on top of the ceramic bowl
- Then SLOWLY pour the water out of the bottle onto the ice. You should see a little tower of ice forming, getting bigger as more water is poured

The science behind what you saw

 The water in the bottle is supercooled, i.e. cooled below its freezing temperature.

- The water molecules turn to ice when they reach the ice cube on top of the bowl because it's easier for the water molecules to turn to ice on top of already-formed crystals. As the ice crystals build on existing ice crystals, they eventually freeze the whole bottle of water as it is being poured.

19
_____

FROZEN 2

What you need

- Teaspoon
- Tablespoon
- Measuring cup
- ¾ cup milk
- ¼ full cream (whipping cream)
- 2 tbsp. granulated sugar
- 1/2 tsp. pure vanilla extract
- 3 cups. ice
- 1/3 cup. salt
- Small plastic ziplock bag
- Large plastic bag

What you do

In the small resealable plastic bag, combine milk, cream, sugar, and vanilla. Push out excess air and seal. In the large plastic bag, combine ice and salt. Place the small bag inside the large bag and shake vigorously for 7 to 10 minutes. You should end up with ice cream (and yes, you can eat it)

The science behind what you saw

Salt lowers the temperature of ice water. Ice always has an outer film of water so it's technically ice water. Putting salt on ice makes it colder. When you add salt to ice), the temperature can drop from freezing or 0 °C to as low as -21 °C. Salt lowers the freezing point of ice, which is why salt is put on icy streets in cold countries

20

MORE ABOUT MOLD

You have probably all seen moldy food. This experiment is about looking for different ways to stop or delay mold from growing on bread

What you need

- 5 slices of white bread
- 5 resealable plastic bags big enough to hold a slice of bread
- Vinegar
- Cooking oil (any)
- Water
- Clothes pegs
- Marking pen or sticky labels

What you do

- Place both hands flat against one slice of bread and place it in a bag. Label the bag with the treatment you used (e.g. unwashed hands)
- Wash your hands well with soap and water, dry them,

43

place both hands flat against another slice of bread, and place it in another bag. Label the bag with the treatment you used (e.g. washed hands)

- Dip one slice in vinegar and put it in another bag. Label the bag with the treatment you used (vinegar)
- Dip one slice in oil and put it in another bag. Label the bag with the treatment you used (oil)
- Dip one slice in water and put it in another bag. Label the bag with the treatment you used (water)
- Close all the bags, and hang them somewhere warm e.g. using clothes pegs to hang them from a string, washing line or coat hanger.
- Check every day, and notice which slice was the first to develop mold.
- Did any of the treatments stop the bread from going moldy?
- What other ways can you think of to stop mould growing on bread?
- Important: When you've finished the experiments, put all the bags in the waste bin without opening them.

The science behind what you saw

Mold grows in damp conditions. You probably found that the bread with water grew mold before the other slices. If you used very dry bread in the other bags you may find that mold was slow to grow, and may not have grown at all Mold can't grow on bread unless mold spores land on it. The fact that bread goes moldy so often indicates that there are many mold spores in the air. Oil and vinegar may prevent mold spores from growing. Can you think of other ways to prevent mold growing on bread that you can test?

21

FANTASTIC PLASTIC

What you need

- A plastic bag (e.g. a ziplock plastic bag or freezer bag)
- Water
- Sharp pencils

Do this experiment outside or next to the kitchen sink.

This experiment needs 2 people

What you do

Fill the bag full of water and check that there are no holes or leaks. One person hold the bag up, using 2 hands, holding tightly , while the other person pokes a pencil straight into the side of the plastic bag (not at an angle) and s it there. Did the water leak out?

If it did, try the experiment again with a different plastic bag.

If it didn't, push another pencil straight into the bag and see what happens. See how many pencils you can push into the bag before it leaks or pops.

Why this happened – the science behind what you saw

Plastic is made of polymers Although you would expect the water to leak when pierced by the pencil, the polymers of the bag's plastic will re-seal around the pencil, so the water doesn't leak out.

FLOWERS BY CHROMATOGRAPHY

What you need

- 5 Coffee filters or filter paper
- 5 plates
- Washable colored marking pens/washable textas – blue, green, red, purple, orange,
- Tap water
- Teaspoon
- Thin ribbon or pipe cleaners

What you do

Flatten each coffee filter onto a plate

Draw a thick lined circle about half way between the middle and edge of each filter paper, using one color for each filter paper

Add a teaspoon of water to the middle of each coffee filter. What happens? Do all the colors act the same way?

Leave the filter papers on the plates to dry

When they have dried, fold them into quarters, and pinch the ends to make a 'stem'. Tie the stems with narrow ribbon or pipe cleaners, and fold back the outer rim of the papers to give a 'flowery' appearance.

The science behind what you saw

The colors should spread out across the filter paper and you should end up with beautiful colored papers, like flowers. Some flowers will have just one color, in others the original color separates into different colors.

The water moves through the paper by what is called capillary action. As it moves it will spread the colors out. If the colors are secondary color (made by mixing 2 other colors) it, may cause them to separate into the colors that made them originally. Chromatography is the name given to the process of separating a mixture by passing it through a substance, when the components travel at different rates, and some of the colors you used will separate out by chromatography. .

23

WALKING WATER

What you need

- Six glasses or clear plastic cups
- Red, blue and yellow food coloring
- Paper towels
- Scissors

What you do

Fill 3 glasses with water and leave the other 3 empty. Add red food coloring to one glass of water, blue coloring to another glass of water and yellow coloring to the third glass of water. Arrange the glasses in a circle, alternating glasses with colored water and empty glasses. Take a half sheet of paper towel and fold it in half lengthwise and in half again lengthwise.

Place one end of a rolled paper towel in the glass with red colouring and place the other end in the empty glass next to it, making a bridge between the two glasses. Then make a bridge with a paper towel from the empty glass into the glass with blue colouring in, and another bridge from the blue glass to another empty glass. Make a bridge from this empty glass into glass with yellow coloring, and from that glass to another empty glass. Then from that empty glass make a bridge to the glass with red colouring. So all the glasses have 2 ends of paper towels in them, connecting them to the glasses next to them

9 Watch what starts happening to the paper towels and the water in the glasses without food coloring.

The science behind what you saw

You would have seen the colored water "walk" over the bridges and into the clear glasses of water. The water moved up through the towels by a process called capillary action. The paper towel is made from fibers and the water travels through the gaps in the fibers. The gaps in the paper towel act like capillary tubes and pull the water upward. The water is able to move upward against gravity because of the attractive forces between the water and the fibers in the paper towel.

Capillary action also helps water climb from a plant's roots to its leaves.

24

TELLING TIME BY THE SUN – MAKE YOUR OWN SUNDIAL

Before people had clocks and watches they used sundials to tell the time. The ancient Egyptians made sundials around 1500 BC.

Because the earth spins around, the sun looks as if it is moving across the sky during the day, so the shadows cast by the sun change during the day. Have a look at your own shadow at different times during the day. What do you notice?

A sundial is made of a thin rod, that casts a shadow onto a flat surface which has markings for each hour of sunlight (so not useful at night)...

What you need to make a sundial

- A sunny place
- Marking pen, pencil, crayon or chalk
- A straw or stick
- Plasticine, playdough (Play-doh) or Blu-Tack
- Paper plate
- Large sheet of paper, wood or cardboard
- Ruler
- Timer, or use the alarm on a phone or alarm clock
- Compass (optional)

Or

If your sunny place is a lawn, or sand (e.g. a beach or sandpit) you just need

- A stick about 2 feet long (about 60 cm).
- Large pebbles or white/cream-colored shells as markers
- Marking pen
- Timer, alarm clock or phone with an alarm
- Compass (optional)

Or

If your sunny place is concrete or asphalt

- Chalk
- A straw or stick
- Plasticine, playdough (Play-doh) or Blu-Tack
- Ruler
- Timer, or use the alarm on a phone or alarm clock
- Compass (optional)

What you do

- Lay the paper/board flat in your chosen sunny space, put the paper plate on it and put a lump of plasticine (or playdough (Play-doh)) in the centre, then push the stick into the plasticine, so it stands sloping slightly towards the North if you live in the Northern Hemisphere (e.g. US, Canada, Europe, UK) or sloping towards the South if you live in the Southern Hemisphere (e.g. Australia, New Zealand, South America, Southern Africa).
- If you don't have a compass to tell you which direction North and South are, start making your sundial at exactly 12.00 noon. At this time, shadows point directly North in the Northern hemisphere and South in the Southern hemisphere. So tilt your stick in the direction of its

shadow at 12.00 noon, draw a line along the shadow (use a ruler to keep the line straight, and write the time '12.00' at the end of the line.

- Then look at your sundial again every hour from then to draw a line and write the time
- Use the timer to remind you to mark the time every hour, or set the alarm on a phone or alarm clock and reset every hour

On grass

- If your space is on grass, you can just push the stick into the soil, sloping it slightly (as described above), and mark the hours with pebbles, without using paper.

On sand

- If your space is on sand (like at the beach or on a sandpit) you can draw lines in the sand or mark the hours with shells or pebbles. Write the time on each shell or pebble with texta or chalk.

On concrete

- If your space is on concrete or other hard surface, and you have chalk, you can just put the plasticine straight onto the concrete, without the paper, and mark the hours with chalk directly on the concrete.

Note that this sundial won't give you exactly the right time every day. For a more accurate sundial, you need to find out the latitude you're in, and be able to measure the angle between your stick and the flat surface below your stick.

The science behind what you saw

The shadow cast by your stick moves slowly in a clockwise direction, throughout the day, as the sun appears to move across the sky from East to West. But actually the earth spins around like a spinning top, so when one half of the earth faces the sun, that half is in sunshine, and the other half is in darkness, and as the earth moves it looks to us as if the sun is moving. As well as spinning round itself (we say it spins on its axis), the earth moves round the sun, taking a year to go all the way round.

When you're hiking or traveling it's often useful to remember that the sun rises in the East and sets in the West, and that midday your shadow points either North if you're in the Northern Hemisphere and South if you're in the Southern Hemisphere, as knowing this can help you find the direction you should be traveling in.

The moon also appears to move across the sky at night in the same direction every night. Like the sun it rises in the East, (so you'll see it low down on the Eastern horizon in the early evening) and sets in the West. But it would be hard to make a moondial. Why?

25

MAKING A SOLAR OVEN

What you need

- Cardboard box – like a pizza box
- Aluminium foil
- Matte black paper or black cardboard
- Clingfilm
- 8 Marshmallows
- 2 plates
- A sunny place
- A teaspoon

What you do

Cover the inside of the box lid with foil and the bottom with black paper.

Place 4 marshmallows on a plate and put the plate inside the box

Place the box so it faces the sun, adjusting the lid so the light is reflected onto the food. Prop the lid open at this position with a stick.

Place the other 4 marshmallows on the second plate and leave outside the box, next to the box.

After 30 minutes (less if it's a very hot day) tap the marshmallows with a teaspoon. Are there any differences between the marshmallows inside and outside the box?

The science behind what happened

You probably found that the marshmallows in the box (solar oven) had melted and were quite squishy when tapped with a spoon, but the marshmallows outside had melted less, and were less squishy.

This is because radiation from the sun (solar radiation) solar radiation from the sun is reflected from the aluminium foil onto the marshmallows, and onto the black paper. The black paper absorbs the heat, helping to heat inside the box.

26

INTO THE FUTURE

Looking back, looking forward

What did you like most about doing these experiments? And did you find out anything you didn't know before?

Scientists discover things by using what's called the scientific method – this involves noticing or observing something, asking questions, thinking of a explanation (a hypothesis) or solutions to problems, doing the experiments to find out if your hypothesis is right, then thinking about the results.

1. *Make an observation* (e.g. after a picnic at the beach, you notice that a lot of sand has fallen into a container of sugar)
2. *Ask a question* e.g. how can I separate a mixture of sugar and sand
3. *Think of a way of doing this (make a hypothesis)* e.g. If you put the mixture in a jug and add hot water to the mixture and stir, the sugar should dissolve but not the sand. The sand should settle to the bottom. Then you could pour off the water into a wide shallow dish, and let it evaporate.
4. *Test your hypothesis* by doing this experiment.

5. *Observe what happen* (You should end up with sand in the jug and sugar in the bowl)
6. Think carefully about (analyze) the results and make a conclusion. You could conclude that because sugar is soluble in water and sand isn't you can make use of this to separate sand from sugar.

You could think of other ways to separate sand from sugar, e.g. if you leave the mixture near an ants' nest the ants may carry away all the sugar but leave the sand.

Scientists have done and are doing amazing things - discovering electricity and how to use it, inventing radios, television phones, computers, finding cures for diseases, not only of people but of animals and plants too, helping stop catching diseases by vaccination, finding out about the universe, and many, many other things.

ABOUT THE AUTHOR

Dr Esther Anderson is a Scientist & Medical writer based in Melbourne Australia who loves doing fun and safe Science experiments with her many Grandkids.

Printed in Great Britain
by Amazon

46907700R00040